DENOMINATIONAL
TRAINING COLLEGES

AND

BOARD SCHOOLS.

BY

The Hon. E. LYULPH STANLEY, M.P.,

(MEMBER OF THE LONDON SCHOOL BOARD.)

LONDON:

JAMES CLARKE & CO., 13 AND 14, FLEET STREET, E.C.

—

1883.

PRICE SIXPENCE.

LONDON :

BARRETT, SONS AND CO., PRINTERS,

BEER LANE, GREAT TOWER STREET, E.C.

DENOMINATIONAL TRAINING COLLEGES AND BOARD SCHOOLS.

———oo⦂o⦂oo———

COMPLAINTS have been frequently made of late as to the inadequacy of the Training College accommodation, and as to the unsatisfactory character of their regulations; and many School Boards throughout the country have gone so far as to memorialise the Education Department on the subject. The facts as to the Training Colleges are briefly as follow:—

The Training Colleges have accommodation for 3,255 students, which is thus distributed :—

	Male.	Female.	Total.
Church of England...	1,047	1,232	2,279
British	190	255	445
Congregational ...	24	31	55
Wesleyan	130	111	241
Roman Catholic ...	70	165	235
	1,461	1,794	3,255

They are practically full; with the exception of the Roman Catholic male college, which had, according to the report of 1881, 30 resident students, with accommodation for 70.

It will be seen that far the largest proportion of the accommodation is in denominational colleges; the only undenominational ones being those of the British and Foreign School Society; though the Congregational College at Homerton may possibly be classed as, to a certain extent, undenominational. But, even including this, the whole undenominational accommodation is only for 500, out of 3,255, or a little over 15 per cent. The Education Department holds, in July, a yearly examination, called the Scholarship Examination, for students desiring to enter college; and the candidates who pass in the first and second classes are eligible for admission.

But the Government Code provides (Art. 93) that: "The candidates are selected and admitted to the examination by the authorities of each college, on their own responsibility."

Usually a candidate makes application for admission to a college beforehand, and either sits for the Government examination at that college, or, by arrangement, at some other college nearer home, where the examination is conducted.

But no person can claim as a right to sit for examination at any college, and the Education Department does not undertake to furnish any independent centre for conducting the examination. There is, therefore, this initial difficulty, that a student desirous of passing the Scholarship Examination may either be excluded altogether, or may be forced to go a considerable distance from his home to some college willing to permit him to sit and be examined. Complaint has been made of this inconvenience from the School Boards of large towns such as Birmingham and Manchester, and it is believed that the Education Department contemplates making some change in the direction of establishing local centres for examination in the large towns, as well as in the training colleges; no such provision was, however, made last July. But after a student has sat and passed he does not acquire a right to admission to college; this depends upon the will of the authorities of the colleges.

In July, 1881, 4,935 candidates were examined, and 3,001 passed successfully. Of these 1,575 went to college and 1,426 failed to get admission; or very nearly one-half. It is clear, therefore, that, unless some rule of admission having reference to the merit of the student be imposed upon the colleges, great injustice may be done to industrious and meritorious students. But, as the colleges regulate their own terms of admission, many of them have other conditions in addition to the passing of the Government examination. Thus it is usual for the See Note A. Church of England Training Colleges to have an examination, not only in Scripture, but also in the Prayer-book and the Church Catechism; and success, or failure, in this examination determines the admission, or exclusion, of the candidate. Again, questions which applicants often have to answer are—"Have you been baptized?" "Have you been confirmed?" "Are you a communicant?" In some cases candidates for admission are expected to accept service in schools of the same denomination as the college. Again, many of the Training Colleges being diocesan, and, to some extent, supported by diocesan contributions, a preference is given to can- See Note B. didates from Church of England Schools in the diocese over applicants from Board Schools, or applicants from outside the diocese, even though the latter may have passed much higher in the Scholarship Examination.

The following facts appear from Part IV. of a Parliamentary Return on Training Colleges in England and Wales, dated 21st June, 1882, and ordered to be printed 24th July, 1882:—*

MALE CANDIDATES FOR SCHOLARSHIP EXAMINATION.

		Bd.	Others.	Not admitted.	Bd.	Others.
1st class ...	318	95	223	49	27	22
2nd class (a)...	181	50	131	47	19	28
(b)...	204	52	152	67	28	39
(c)...	369	87	282	191	59	132
	1,072	284	788	354	133	221

Thus 718 went to college, out of 1,072 who passed, or about 67 per cent.; but whereas, of the candidates who were not from Board Schools, 568 out of 778 went to college, or about 72 per cent.; of the candidates from Board Schools, only 151 out of 284, or about 53 per cent., went to college. If Board School candidates had See Note

---

* Part IV. is not printed, but is deposited in the Library of the House of Commons.

been admitted in the same proportion as the others, 204 would have gone to college, or 53 more than were admitted; and this disproportion, unfavourable to the Board Schools, was not owing to the bad quality of the candidates; for, whereas the total of successful Board School candidates was about 26½ per cent. of the whole number, in the first class the proportion was about 30 per cent., while in the lowest section of the second class it was only 24 per cent.; showing that the Board School candidates passed generally higher than the others.

If we take the female candidates at the Scholarship Examinations, we find the following facts:—

		Passed.		Not admitted.		
		Bd.	Others.		Bd.	Others.
1st class ...	634	221	413	163	82	81
2nd class (a)...	363	104	259	187	69	118
(b)...	391	125	266	255	99	156
(c)...	541	138	403	468	134	334
	1,929	588	1,341	1,073	384	689

Thus 855 went to college out of 1,929 who passed, or about 44 per cent.; but whereas, of the candidates who were not from Board Schools, 651 out of 1,340 went to college, or about 48 per cent.; of the candidates from Board Schools, 204 out of 588 went to college, or about 34 per cent. Had the Board School candidates gone to college in the same proportion as the others, 272 would have gone, or 68 more than were admitted.

The successful Board School candidates were 30 per cent. of the whole; but in the first class they were nearly 35 per cent. of the whole; and in the lowest division of the second class they were only 25½ per cent. of the whole. Thus among the female, as among the male, candidates for admission those from Board Schools did materially better than the others, and yet were admitted in a much lower proportion.

Had those who passed in the third division of the second class been excluded from college, and had the 855 vacancies been filled up exclusively from the 1,388 who passed in the first class and the first two divisions of the second class in equal proportions from Board School candidates and from others, out of the 450 successful Board School candidates, being 32·4 per cent. of the whole, 277 students should have been admitted, or 73 more than were admitted; while 578 instead of 651 should have been admitted from the voluntary schools. These figures show clearly that the authorities of the training colleges give a preference to applicants coming from denominational schools over those coming from Board Schools, and this is not denied by the authorities.

The Roman Catholic colleges may be set on one side, as it will be an event of the greatest rarity for any one who has passed the Scholarship Examination and who is not a Roman Catholic to seek entrance to a Roman Catholic college. But the Wesleyan colleges and the Church of England colleges profess to be available for the training of the general run of those desirous of pursuing the profession of teacher. They claim, however, as having been constructed chiefly at the expense of their own denominations, and being still partially maintained by them, to See Note B. have a moral, as well as a legal, right to exercise a discrimination in favour of their own denomination. And this claim need not be disputed if, in the first place, they did not receive very large annual contributions from the State, and, secondly, if there were plenty of opportunities elsewhere to get training.

If the denominational training colleges are to be treated as correlative to the denominational schools, then they are more numerous than the needs of their schools demand. Thus the Church of England schools had in 1881 about 52 per cent. of all the children in average attendance; and for these their proportion of the training college accommodation would be 1,693 places, instead of 2,279 places. The Wesleyans had 4·2 per cent. of the children, and the equivalent training college accommodation would be 137 places, instead of 241. The Roman Catholics, with 5·3 per cent of the children, should have 172 places instead of 235. This would give a total reduction of 753 places in the denominational colleges, in order to supply an equivalent extension to training colleges in harmony with the Board School and British system, and likely to give equal facilities to pupil teachers coming from that class of school. But, as a matter of fact, the Board system is growing year by year, and such an adjustment, even if fair now, would cease to be fair in a very few years. It is some-times objected that it does not follow that, because students come from Board Schools, they are not members of the Church of England, or Wesleyans, and it is contended that the large number of Board School candidates who now go to the denominational colleges proves that these colleges are, in fact, suitable for the training of teachers coming from and intending to go to Board Schools. The answer to this is—first, the candidates have no choice. If they are to get the advantage of training, a very large number of them must put up with the regulations of the denominational training colleges, or remain untrained. Thus in the report of the Education Department for 1881-2 it is stated (p. xvi.) that, out of 369 Board pupil teachers, 146 entered denominational colleges—that is about 40 per cent. But these very figures show that the Board School can-didates, at any rate, greatly prefer the undenominational colleges ; for, whereas the denominational colleges are about 86 per cent. of the whole, we find only 40 per cent. of the Board scholars going to them, and it is notorious that in many cases they go to the denomina-tional colleges only because they know they cannot pass high enough to get into such colleges as the Borough Road, or Stockwell. It is clear then that, even granting that the denominational colleges should still be subsi-dized, in the interest of the denominational schools, and granting that the State has no reason to be dissatisfied with their efficiency, or management, still their accom-modation is excessive ; having regard to the changed conditions of our public Elementary Education, and it is likely to become more so as every year passes by.

The Education Department endeavours to minimise the evil of this state of things in the report for 1881-2, for at page xvi. they glance at the complaints that are being made, and suggest some palliatives ; but the Department quite fails to recognize the seriousness of the complaints and the necessity for much more thorough remedies. Every year the Education Department republishes substantially the same paragraph, estimating the annual waste in the teaching body at 6 per cent., and complacently noting the large number of teachers who are introduced into the profession outside of the training colleges. Occasionally the cry has been raised that too many teachers are trained and that there is a glut of them. An attempt is made to suggest this by the statement that on April, 1882, 154 students who passed the certificate examination were still unplaced. This number was reduced by June to 61 ; exclusive of 24 who had refused situations, and this is out of 1,500 who passed; and, again, 18 of these unplaced teachers passed in the third division. As to all of them, that they are unplaced is their own fault ; for the London School Board is constantly advertising for, and failing to get, properly qualified teachers, and that Board offers salaries which are certainly not illiberal. But what are the teachers whom the Education Department brings in competition with those trained mainly at the expense of the nation? Last Christmas, for 1,500 trained teachers, 2,094 acting teachers were certificated. Of these 1,960 were passed, after an examination on the first year's papers, and of these 847 passed in the third, and 641 in the fourth division—very nearly as many as the whole number of trained teachers. Besides these, the Education Department actually recognizes ex-pupil teachers as fit to take charge, single-handed, of small village schools of less than 60 average attendance. Of these, since 1871, the Department has recognized 3,551. This tolerance, or rather encouragement, of inferior teachers for small schools is expressly justified on the score of expense. Thus the report of the

Education Department for 1881-2, states (page xxi.): "A considerable number of teachers who have not passed through the training colleges will always be required for service in the small schools throughout the country. . . . The salaries obtained, even by female teachers, after two years' training are beyond the means of managers of small schools." No doubt, in the rural districts, where the inhabitants are determined to exclude a School Board, and yet are unwilling to pay the cost of an efficient school, this boon, in the form of the recognition of ex-pupil teachers, is most welcome; but, in the interests of education, these young people, whose ages range from 18 to 26, and who have had nothing beyond a rudimentary instruction themselves, ought never to be recognized as teachers, except in schools where they will be under the supervision of a trained and experienced head teacher, competent to supervise their methods and further their studies.

The requirements of elementary education in Scotland are recognized in a far more liberal spirit. There are 409,966 children in average attendance, and 850 students in training. Assuming that this is slightly in excess of the requirements of Scotland, and deducting the 62 who found employment in England, and the 71 unplaced in April, there remain 717 students in training to supply teaching power for 410,000 children. At the same rate there ought to be more than 5,000 students in training in England for the 2,863,000 children in average attendance, instead of which there are only 3,121. Again, in Scotland only 27·87 per cent. of the masters, and 23·98 per cent. of the mistresses, are untrained; while in England 29·75 per cent. of the masters, and 49·32 per cent. of the mistresses are untrained.

But it must be remembered that in Scotland there are no conflicting denominational interests to be protected, and therefore the question of the efficiency of the schools comes first in the minds of the people, and consequently in the consideration of the Education Department. In England we are handicapped with what is called the Voluntary,

·but should be called the Denominational, system; in the interest of which the whole standard of education is depressed. Letters from the Education Department to School Boards often openly put forth this need for protection of the interests of voluntary schools, as a reason why some application should be refused.

It is alleged that there is enough training accommodation. By the example of Scotland we have shown that it is not the case. It is alleged that denominational training colleges are the correlative of denominational schools. It has been shown that from that point of view their proportion of the whole accommodation is excessive. It is alleged that no interference with their religious exclusiveness can be made without breaking faith with those who have founded them. But their annual maintenance is almost entirely at the public expense. Only about thirteen per cent. of their yearly cost is defrayed by the subscriptions and endowments of their voluntary supporters, about fourteen per cent. from the payments of the students, and seventy-three per cent. from the parliamentary grants. There is no See Note B. obligation to keep up this subsidy indefinitely, especially in the greatly altered condition of elementary education, and the financial position of teachers at the present day. Nor is the teaching given at the present training colleges so good that we cannot reasonably expect better. The instruction may be better than can be acquired by ex-pupil teachers of an evening, but is yet most unsatisfactory. This arises, partly from the inferior quality of many of the students, who have been admitted for denominational rather than educational reasons, and partly from the income of some of the colleges being limited, which prevents their doing justice to their students.

What then is the remedy? Mr. Mundella offers us See Note D one or two more training colleges, managed in the same irresponsible way as the existing ones under private committees, and not all of them undenominational. He has also thrown out vague hints of Day Training Colleges in London, to which we may suppose some Government subsidy would be afforded; but this hint has not yet been transformed into any definite proposal.

The School Boards which have complained of the grievance have not, as a rule, formulated any definite remedy. Some ask, as a minimum, for the admission into existing colleges of candidates in the order of merit according to the Scholarship Examination, and without regard to denominational distinctions, subject, of course, to proper certificates of good character. This would leave the compulsory religious teaching within the college as it is. But how unsatisfactory to admit a Baptist, a Quaker, or a Unitarian into a Church of England College, such as Whitelands or Salisbury, and then compel them to attend the chapel service, to receive the communion, to follow lectures on Church History and on the Prayer Book, from an Anglican, and possibly a very High Church, standpoint! Such a thing is not attempted at Oxford or Cambridge; where the College life is also domestic, and where, nevertheless, the fullest liberty of conscience is accorded to Nonconformists. But the majority of the colleges, it seems, are prepared to resist, not only the conscience clause within their walls, but even the obligation to admit in order of merit. They claim full liberty to reject not merely on moral or religious grounds, but even on what I may call capricious grounds. A Church of England training college [See Note D.] lately rejected a candidate from a Sheffield school because he was not tall enough to join the local volunteer corps! And the London School Board have on record a [See Return under Note C.] case where a young man was refused at another diocesan training college on account of his height.

If, then, existing colleges wish to retain their absolute liberty of selection, and of internal management, the nation should either give power to School Boards to found other and undenominational colleges side by side with the existing ones, which would probably be the best course, or should suppress some of the accommodation in existing training colleges, in order that it might be transferred to new colleges, to be founded by School Boards.

Those School Boards which are not large enough to found a college for themselves might be associated within the limit of a county, or of two or three counties, to found one in common. In any case the present scandal—for it is no less—should cease, and the door of admission to a national and unsectarian system of education should not be mainly under the control of one exclusive Church, which has power to refuse those of another communion, and to enforce its theological teaching on all who would enter. Justice to religious freedom, justice to educational efficiency, alike require that a substantial change should be made; and if the Education Department has not the courage, or the sense of what is due to the rights of conscience, or the desire for thoroughly efficient teaching which we have a right to expect, it will be the duty of the various progressive forces which are working in the country, and which can influence Parliament, to agitate till greater wisdom and greater liberality can penetrate even to Whitehall. We claim for the education of the people that its most complete efficiency should be the first object of our rulers, and that no vested interests, no sectarian objects, should stand in its way. In many other matters—such as the character of school buildings, the area allotted to each child, the indulgence with which results are tested—the Education Department deals out one measure to School Boards, and another to Voluntary Schools. In all these matters we expect, and if need be we shall demand, that henceforward the interests of the children shall be considered, and those alone. Meantime, we ask for the fullest opportunity for efficient and unsectarian training for all those who are willing and fitted to enter on the responsible career of teachers in the elementary schools of the nation.

C

NOTES ON DENOMINATIONAL TRAINING COLLEGES.

THE Voluntary Training Colleges dealt with in the foregoing pages for the training of Teachers of Elementary public schools receiving State-aid are thirty-nine in number. Of these thirty-four are strictly denominational. They originated in private effort, and are under sectarian management, which is irresponsible to the State : and the Government Code provides that the authorities of each college may settle their own terms of admission.

The Colleges may be classified denominationally as follows :—

28 CHURCH OF ENGLAND.
   In these the students are examined in the Bible and Prayer Book and the inquiries relating to religion are such as indicate that they are expected to be members of the Church of England.

2 WESLEYAN COLLEGES.
   The inquiries to candidates for admission are of a somewhat rigorous character, and imply that inmates are members of the Wesleyan Methodist Society,* and formerly it was stipulated that students intended to teach in Wesleyan schools ; but much public attention having been drawn to this subject this condition has been modified.

1 CONGREGATIONAL COLLEGE.
   There is no test, but inquiry is made as to the religious character and the denomination of applicants.

---

* On the 8th December, 1881, a letter from the Rev. Dr. Rigg, Principal of the Wesleyan Training College, Westminster, and the Rev. G. O. Bate, Principal of the Wesleyan Training College, Southlands, Battersea, pointing out inaccuracies in the return relative to tests, given on page 16, was submitted to the London School Board. In this letter it was stated that the rule in regard to future service instead of being as follows—" Before being admitted to residence the candidate has to sign a declaration of which the following undertaking is one of the clauses :—' That when the period of my training in the College has expired, I will serve as an assistant or as a principal teacher in a Public Elementary Day School connected with the Wesleyan Education Committee, if I am required so to do by that Committee ; ' would be ' That when the period of my training in the College has expired, I will serve as an Assistant or as a Principal Teacher in a Public Elementary School.' "

3 ROMAN CATHOLIC COLLEGES.

Two only have made returns relative to tests, but it may be assumed that all three are strictly denominational and exclusive.

5 UNDENOMINATIONAL COLLEGES.

These are of the British and Foreign School Society type, and impose no ecclesiastical tests and have no religious examination, though ministerial certificates as to moral and religious character are required.

In May, 1881, the Metropolitan Board Teachers' Association forwarded to the London School Board the following resolution :—

" That, in the opinion of this meeting the principles upon which the Training Colleges were founded having been determined prior to the rise of Board Schools, such reforms in the existing scheme of training have become necessary as will remove the special disabilities under which the Board candidates labour, and secure for them the same rights and privileges of admission to colleges as are enjoyed by the competitors from denominational schools."

This resolution having been referred to the School Management Committee of the Board, that Committee applied to each of the training colleges for copies of the form of application for admission, and some of them having been received and considered, the Committee reported, recommending that the Board should present a memorial to the Education Department on the subject.

In January, 1882, the Board, after lengthy discussion, resolved as follows :—

" The School Board call the attention of the Education Department to the conditions of admission to the existing training colleges, and to the difficulties which impede the admission of Board school pupil teachers to the full educational advantages of training, and urges the Education Department to take such steps as may seem to them necessary in order to secure the Board school pupil teachers equal advantages for training with those who come from denominational schools."

It was also resolved to forward to the Department, a return of the conditions, &c., of entering the colleges.

NOTE A.
TESTS FOR ADMISSION TO TRAINING COLLEGES.

TESTS.—The London School Board Return obtained as above narrated, included information respecting (1) any preliminary condition or inquiry of an ecclesiastical character that is made before the admission of a candidate into College ; and (2) the nature of the Scripture or religious examination (if any) which the candidates are required to attend before their admission. The following tabulated statement contains the result :—

RETURN WITH REFERENCE TO PUPIL TEACHERS' ADMISSION INTO TRAINING COLLEGES.

College.	For Masters or Mistresses.	Whether any preliminary condition or inquiry of an ecclesiastical character is made.	Nature of Scripture or religious Examination (if any) before entrance.
		BRITISH AND FOREIGN SCHOOL SOCIETY'S COLLEGES.	
Bangor	Masters	Testimonial required of moral and religious character from Minister of Church or Chapel.	None.
Borough Road	Masters	Form to be filled up by Minister of Church or Chapel as to religious character.	None.
Stockwell ...	Mistresses	Ditto	None.
Darlington ...	Mistresses	Ditto	None.
Swansea ...	Mistresses	Ditto	
		NATIONAL SOCIETY'S COLLEGES.	
Battersea ...	Masters	... ...	Old and New Testament and Prayer Book (N.S.).
Carmarthen ...	Masters	Certificate from Clergyman.—Certificate of Baptism. — Inquiry made: Have you been confirmed? If not, are you desirous of being confirmed? Are you a communicant?	Ditto.
St. Mark's ...	Masters	Certificate or proof of Baptism.—Recommendation of character from Clergyman. — Questions as to confirmation and being a communicant.	Ditto. Failure in this examination does not necessarily exclude.
Tottenham ...	Mistresses	Inquiry: are you a member of the Church of England?	Old and New Testament and Prayer Book (N.S.).
Whitelands ...	Mistresses	Inquiry: Have you been confirmed? Are you a communicant? or do you propose to be?—Baptismal Certificate required.—*After training,* supposed to *educate children* in the *principles of the Church of England.*	Old and New Testament and Prayer Book (N.S.) Candidates for admission *must pass.* Great importance is attached to the results of the Diocesan Examination.
		CHURCH OF ENGLAND TRAINING COLLEGES.	
Cheltenham ...	Masters & Mistresses	Inquiry to be answered by Clergyman or Manager: Is he (or she) a member of the Church of England? Confirmed? Communicant?	Old and New Testament and Prayer Book(N.S.). Candidates *must present themselves* for this Examination.

College.	For Masters or Mistresses.	Whether any preliminary condition or inquiry of an ecclesiastical character is made.	Nature of Scripture or religious Examination (if any) before entrance.
Peterborough...	Mistresses	Inquiry to be answered by Candidate: Have you been confirmed?—Certificate of Baptism required.	Old and New Testament and Prayer Book (N.S.). Candidates required *to pass* this Examination.
Carnarvon ...	Masters	No return received.	

DIOCESAN COLLEGES.

College.	For Masters or Mistresses.	Whether any preliminary condition or inquiry of an ecclesiastical character is made.	Nature of Scripture or religious Examination (if any) before entrance.
Culham	Masters	Certificate of character from Clergyman or Managers.—Certificate of Baptism required.—Teachers make *declaration* that they will follow *profession of Church teacher in Elementary Schools.*	Old and New Testament and Prayer Book (N.S.). ...
Durham... ...	Masters & Mistresses	Certificate from Clergyman as to character and certificate of Baptism required.—Candidates *must* be *communicants.*	Old and New Testament and Prayer Book.
Exeter	Masters	Certificate of Baptism required and one from Clergyman as to character.	Old and New Testament and Prayer Book (N.S.). *Examination compulsory.*
Saltley	Masters	... ...	Old and New Testament and Prayer Book (N.S.).
Winchester ...	Masters	Inquiry to be answered by Candidates: Are you a member of the Church of England? Confirmed? Communicant?—*Candidates who do not answer these questions are admitted, and sometimes even failures in the Scripture Examination.*	Old and New Testament and Prayer Book. ...
York	Masters	Certificate of character from Clergyman or Manager and Master.	Old and New Testament and Prayer Book (N.S.). *20 per cent. of students admitted have not passed this Examination, but all Candidates must attend Scripture Lectures and Lectures on Prayer Book.*
Bristol	Mistresses	Certificate of character, and attention to religious character from Clergyman and certificate of Baptism required.	Old and New Testament and Prayer Book. *Candidates must pass this examination.*
Lincoln	Mistresses	... ...	Old and New Testament and Prayer Book (N.S.). *Failure at this Examination excludes.*
Norwich ...	Mistresses	Certificate from Clergyman that candidate has been baptised, confirmed, and is a constant communicant?	Old and New Testament and Prayer Book. Preference given to those Candidates who pass. Board Teachers are admitted.

College.	For Masters or Mistresses.	Whether any preliminary condition or inquiry of an ecclesiastical character is made.	Nature of Scripture or religious Examination (if any) before entrance.
Oxford	Mistresses	Certificate from Clergyman and Certificate of Baptism.—Candidates *must be Communicants of Church of England.*—Inquiries: Has she been confirmed and is she a communicant?	Old and New Testament and Prayer Book (N.S.).
Ripon	Mistresses	Candidates to answer inquiry: Has she been confirmed? Is she a communicant? and to furnish a Certificate of Baptism.	Old and New Testament and Prayer Book (N.S.). *Candidates must pass this Examination.*
Warrington ...	Mistresses	Baptismal certificate required, and inquiry: Are you confirmed and a communicant?	
Home & Col....	Mistresses	Questions to be answered: Are you a member of the Church of England? and have you been confirmed?	Old and New Testament and Prayer Book (N.S.).
Chichester ...	Mistresses	Candidates asked: If been confirmed? and if a communicant? Not *obliged* to be *answered in the affirmative.* Candidates not answering have been accepted.	Old and New Testament and Prayer Book (N.S.). Candidates admitted who have not gone in for this Examination.
Salisbury ...	Mistresses	Date of Baptism required and answers to questions. Have you been confirmed? Are you a communicant? Certificate from Clergyman required.	Old and New Testament and Prayer Book. Failure excludes.
Truro	Mistresses	Question: Has she been for certain confirmed and a regular attendant at your Church?	Old and New Testament and Prayer Book (N.S.).
Chester	Masters	No return received.	
Brighton ...	Mistresses	No return received.	
Derby	Mistresses	No return received.	
Bishop Stortford	Mistresses	No return received.	
		ROMAN CATHOLIC COLLEGES.	
Liverpool ...	Mistresses	... ...	Examination in religious knowledge for those who have not passed a satisfactory examination during last year of apprenticeship
Hammersmith	Masters	For Candidates from Catholic Schools and other approved Candidates.	Ditto. Ditto.
Wandsworth ...	Mistresses	No return received.	

College.	For Masters or Mistresses.	Whether any preliminary condition or inquiry of an ecclesiastical character is made.	Nature of Scripture or religious Examination (if any) before entrance.
		WESLEYAN TRAINING COLLEGES.	
Southlands ... Westminster ...	Mistresses } Masters }	Candidates to produce satisfactory report as to *religious character* from the Wesleyan *Methodist Superintendent* Minister of the Circuit.—Questions asked : Are you a Member of the Wesleyan Methodist Society ? When did you receive your ticket ? If not, are you a Member of any other Christian Communion ? Do you cordially approve of the doctrines and discipline of the Wesleyan Methodist Society ? If admitted will you faithfully observe its Rules ? If required by the Committee will you *continue as a teacher connected* with the *Wesleyan Education Committee ?*	Old and New Testament and Conference Catechism. The Committee at liberty, if all vacancies are not filled up, to admit Candidates of other denominations, so long as they are satisfied with religious character.
		CONGREGATIONAL COLLEGE.	
Homerton ...	Masters & Mistresses	Following Questions to be answered : What are the name and the denomination of the Minister you are in the habit of hearing ? Are you a Member of a Christian Church ? If so, of what Church ?—Questions asked of the Clergyman or Minister of the Church attended : Does the Candidate attend your Church regularly ? Is the Candidate a communicant of your Church ?	No Examination in religious knowledge.

In all Church of England and Diocesan Training Colleges, Candidates are examined in the Old and New Testament and in the Book of Common Prayer ; but at York, Saltley, and Chichester Candidates are admitted without passing this Examination.

N.S. shows that the Examination is conducted by the National Society.

NOTE B.

INCOME OF DENOMINATIONAL TRAINING COLLEGES.

The Report of the Committee of the Council of Education, 1881-82, shows the income of Denominational Training Colleges to be, from various sources, as follows :—

Grants from the State £112,908 4 3
Endowments and Exhibitions 1,374 11 11
Voluntary Subscriptions and Donations, individuals, church and chapel collections, &c. } £7,769 6 11
Diocesan Boards and other charitable Boards 11,164 10 1
18,933 17 0
Students' Fees and Payments 21,276 2 11
£154,492 16 1

which shows that 73·08 per cent. of income is derived from the State; ·89 per cent. from endowments; 12·26 per cent. from voluntary contributions; and 13·77 per cent. from the students.

The same Blue-book (page 493) shows that the original cost of building Denominational Training Colleges has been as follows :—

	Voluntarily Subscribed.			State-aid.			Total.		
	£	s.	d.	£	s.	d.	£	s.	d.
Church of England ...	195,685	14	2	97,474	10	3	293,160	4	5
British	40,425	9	7	12,203	7	6	52,628	17	1
Wesleyan	33,101	9	3	5,049	10	0	38,150	19	3
Congregational ...	......			......			......		
Roman Catholic ...	9,630	0	8	3,900	0	0	13,530	0	8
Total	278,842	13	8	118,627	7	9	397,470	1	5

That is 29·85 per cent. of the total first cost of buildings has been defrayed out of public funds. These figures, however, apply only to original cost. The Blue-book, on page xix., gives a further statement.

The Training Colleges have been established at a cost of £634,755 8s. 5½d., distributed as follows :—

Training Colleges.	Grant from the State.			Voluntary Contributions.		
	£	s.	d.	£	s.	d.
Church of England...	92,613	15	3	271,185	16	1¼
Roman Catholic	3,900	0	0	66,601	8	4
Wesleyan	5,049	10	0	68,804	18	9
British	12,920	0	0	80,080	0	0
Congregational	......			33,600	0	0
	£114,483	5	3	£520,272	3	2¼

It is not obvious what these figures include, but they probably embrace the erection of chapels and other purely denominational structures, and possibly some expenditure on repairs and improvements of existing buildings.

NOTE *C.*

PUPIL TEACHERS UNABLE TO GAIN ADMISSION.

The London School Board has issued a Return showing that, during a period of four years, 105 qualified persons had been unable to gain admission to Denominational Training Colleges. The following is the Return :—

(B) TEACHERS WHO HAVE PASSED IN THE SECOND CLASS, BUT WHO HAVE BEEN UNABLE TO GAIN ADMISSION INTO COLLEGES.

MALES (SECOND CLASS).

Name of Teacher.	School.	Colleges applied to.	Reasons for refusal.	No. on List.
Burnett, G. D. ...	Medburn Street ...	Bat.	Full	403
Yeeles, J.	High St., Shadwell..	Win.	Not a Mem. of C. of E.	462
,, ...	,, ...	Cul., Peter., Ban., Dur., Carm., Chest.	Full	
Mattinson, W. M. ...	Southampton Street	Bat.	Full	468
Levens, J. T. ...	Angler's Gardens ...	Ban.	Too low, out of Wales	525
,, ...	,, ...	Hom.	Full	
Raby, W. A. ...	Harper Street ...	Boro'	Not high enough ...	540
,, ...	,, ...	West.	Not Wesleyan ...	
,, ...	,, ...	Win.	Not Church ...	
,, ...	,, ...	Hom.	Did not sit there ...	
,, ...	,, ...	Chelt.	Too low	
Williams, R. E. ...	Jessop Road ...	Boro'	Not high enough ...	549
Redman, E. T. ...	Bowling Green Road	Boro', York, Cul.	Full	664
,, ...	,, ...	Win., Carm.	Asked if Candidate was Mem. of C. of E. Replied in negative. They then wrote that they were full.	
,, ...	,, ...	Darl., Hom., Salt., West. ...	Full	
Grisby, C. E. ...	Ricardo Street ...	Boro'	Too low	732
Hickman, J. F. ...	James Street ...	Boro'	Too low	822
Hemmings, J. W...	Saunders Road ...	Boro'	Too low	852
,, ...	,, ...	Cul., Hom., West. ...	Full	
Payne, W. Z. ...	Keeton's Road ...	Exet.	On acc. of height...	862
Lloyd, E. B. ...	Shap Street... ...	Cul.	Too low	972
,, ...	,, ...	Hom., Carm.	Full	
Cuff, G. F. ...	Boundary Lane ...	Boro'	Too low	1038

FEMALES (FIRST CLASS).

Name of Teacher.	School.	Colleges applied to.	Reasons for Refusal.	No. on List.
Johnson, J. ...	Blundell Street ...	Stoc.	No room ; left the profession	414
Browne, B. ...	St. John's, Limehse.	Stoc., Hom., Bright. ...	No room	438
Green, G. ...	Laystall Street ...	Stoc.	No vacancy ...	504
Orton, R. J. ...	Turin Street ...	Stoc., Oxford ...	No vacancy ...	530
Waldron, A. ...	Wellington Street ...	Stoc.	Too low	546
,, ...	,, ...	Hom., H. & C., Sth. ...	Did not sit at these Colleges ...	
Hammond, A. ...	Victory Place ...	Stoc.	Too low	583
,, ...	,, ...	B. Stor.	No vacancy ...	
,, ...	,, ...	Chelt., Lin., Bris., Hom. Bright.	Filled by 1st class who sat at Coll...	
Holloway, C. E. ...	Princes Street ...,	Hom.	College full ...	589
Cockburn, F. C. ...	Albany Row ...	Stock	No vacancy ...	608

FEMALES (SECOND CLASS).

Name of Teacher.	School.	Colleges applied to.	Reasons for Refusal.	No. on List.
Hawes, G. ...	Teesdale Street ...	Hom.	Too low	658
Graham, J. E. ...	Hawley Crescent ...	Stoc., Hom., Bright., Nor., Sth., White., Sal., Brist., B. Stor., Dur.	Too low and no vacancies	683
Jenkyn, M. M. ...	Cayley Street ...	Hom., Sth., Darl.	No room	683
Rose, E.	Melvin Road ...	Hom., Darl., Swan., Sth., A. & C.	No room	730
,, ...	,,	White.	No room and Scrip. Ex. not passed	
Smith, F. M. ...	Horseferry Road ...	Stoc., Hom., Swan., Darl.	No room for 2nd class	730
Roby, H. M. ...	Brewhouse Lane ...	Hom., Darl., Swan., Sth. ...	No vacancies ...	709
Thompson, J. ...	Sumner Road ...	Stoc., Hom., H. & C., Sth., Darl., Swan.	Colleges full ...	760
Mackay, J. ...	Marlboro' Road ...	Hom., Chic., Chelt , Tott. ...	Too low	839
Hunter, E. ...	High St., Bromley...	Tott., Nor.	Too low	843
Smurdon, M. J. ...	Rolls Road	Hom., Bat., Der., Chic., Rip., Chelt., Nor., Oxf., Lin., Liv., Brist., War., B. Stor., Salis., Dur., Truro, Darl.	No vacancies ...	865
,, ...	,, ...	Wand:	R. C. College ...	
Peddar, G. ...	St. Paul's Road ...	Swan., Bright., Oxf. ...	Preference given to students who sat there	865
,, ...	,, ...	Stoc., Sth., H. & C., Brist.	No room	
Weight, N. ...	Globe Terrace ...	Stoc.	No room	865
Cashmore, A. A. ...	Bowling Green Lane	Stoc., Sth., Tott., Salis., Bright., B. Stor.	No room	880
Wilkins, F. ...	Wellington Street ...	Stoc., Hom., Truro... ...	No room	890
,, ...	,, ...	Bat., H. & C., Bris., Darl.	Only take their own students	

Name of Teacher.	School.	Colleges applied to.	Reasons for Refusal.	No. on List.
Rhodes, E. ...	North Bow ...	Stoc., H. & C., Sth., Whit., B. Stor., Bright., Darl., Swan.	Full	890
Bayley, L. ...	Gloucester Road ...	Dur., Swan.	No room. Denomination unsatis.	922
,, ...	,, ...	Stoc., Darl., Swan.... ...	Full	
Grinstead, E. ...	Southampton Street	Darl., Dur., Stoc., Swan., Oxf., Hom., B. Stor.	No vacancy ...	922
,, ...	,, ...	Tott.	No reply	
Jackson, S. ...	Albany Row ...	Stoc.	No vacancy ...	941
House, S. E. ...	Marlboro' Street ...	Hom.	Health Cert. ...	941
,, ...	,, ..	B. Stor.	Not satisfactory Scrip. Exam.	
,, ...	,, ...	Oxf., Chic., Bright... ...	No vacancy ...	
Fitch, E.	Hornsey Road ...	Whit., Nor., Bright., Bris., Salis., Chic.	No vacancy ...	980
Black, E.	Nightingale Street ...	Swan., Hom., Sth., Aber., Glas., Edin.	No room	980
Gaster, F. ...	Northey Street ...	Bright.	Not 1st class ...	985
Kitchen, A. ...	High St., S. Newgtn.	Hom.	Too low on list ...	990
Able, C.	Waterloo Street ...	Stoc., B. Stor., Bright., Chic., Darl., H. & C., Nor., Sth., Tott.	Already full ...	997
Merryless, M. J. ...	Medburn Street ...	Stoc.	Too low	1013
Early, M. A. ..	Nightingale Street ...	Stoc.	Too low	1050
Goddard, E. ...	Vittoria Place ...	Stoc.	Too low	1067
Smith, A. ...	Tower Street ...	Stoc., Hom.	No vacancy ...	1094
French, F. ...	Barnet Street ...	Hom., Bright.	Full	1116
Marks, J. ...	James Street West...	Hom.	Too low	1127
Humphrey, A. ...	Fleet Road	H. & C., Bris., Bright., Chelt., Stoc., Nor., and 6 others	All full	1153
Goodwin, L. ...	Upper North Street	Tott., Stoc., Bright. ...	Full	1164
Horne, J.	Westmoreland Road	Sth., Hom.	Full	1174
Gilbert, L. ...	Keeton's Road ...	H.&C., Truro., Salis., Derby, Lin., Nor., and 8 others	1. Too low. No vacancies	1174
Martin, L. E. ...	Rotherhithe N. Rd.	Bright., Salis., Bris., Darl., Dur., Oxf., Nor., Edin.	1. No reason assigned. All vacancies filled	1211
Cook, A. G. ...	Plumstead Road ...	Chelt., Truro, Chic., Bris., Nor., Swan.	All vacancies filled	1213
Firman, A. A. ...	Wornington Road ...	Tott., Nor., Oxf., Brig., Ripon., H. & C., and 10 others	No room	1230
Jones, H. J. ...	Randall Place ...	Stoc., Sth., H. & C., Tott., Hom.	1. Too low. Others filled by their own candidates	1243
Watson, N. H. ...	Winstanley Road ...	Tott.	No room	1243
Morton, R. ...	Wolverley Street ...	Hom., Darl....	Too low	1247
,, ...	,, ...	Bright., Chic., H. & C., Tott.	No room ... ,,	
King, M. A. ...	East St., Kennington	Hom.	Too low	1303
Dawes, A. ...	Shap Street... ...	Oxf., Tott.	Full	1303
Jones, E.	Upper Earl Street ...	Stoc.	Too low	1325
Long, J.	Belvedere Place ...	Stoc.	No room	1344

Name of Teacher.	School.	Colleges applied to.	Reasons for refusal.	No. on List.
Ames, E.	Lamb Lane	Tott., H. & C., Hom., Stoc.	Full	1388
Martin, H. S. ...	Bolingbroke Road ...	Bright., Lin., Bris., B. Stor., Salis., Hom.	Failed in Scrip. No vacancies	1446
Fauke, E. M. ...	Bellenden Road ...	Bright.	Too low	1467
Taylor, M. ...	Harper Street ...	Hom.	Too low	1484
Bacon, E. ...	High Street, Bromley	Tott.	No room	1485
Leutchford, A. M.	New Park Road ...	Stoc.	No room	1497
Laker, L.	Galley Wall Road ...	*Every College*	No vacancy ...	1513
Fisher, A. ...	Canonbury Road ...	B. Stor., Tott., Lin., Nor., Sth., Dur.	1. Not examined in Scrip. ; 2-6. No vacancy	1541
Dover, S.	Hanbury Street ...	Bright.	Too low	1554
Edwards, A. E. ...	Caley Street ...	Hom., Dar., Sth., Swan. ...	No room ; 4. No answer	1554
Williams, E. E. ...	Turin Street ...	Hom., H. & C., Tru., Chelt., Chic., B. Stor.	Full	1566
Samuel, A. ...	Mansfield Place ...	Tott., Hom., B. Stor., Nor., Bright., War., Stoc., Darl., Chelt.	No room	1566
Green, E. ...	London Fields ...	Hom.	No room	1581
Dodge, A. ...	Charles Street, S.E.	Hom.	No room	1581
Wynne, A. ...	Baker Street ...	Bright., B. Stor., Sal., Tott.	No vacancy ...	1598
Nicholls, M. ...	Hargrave Park Road	Hom.	Not 1st class ...	1618
Fane, E. ...	Tennyson Road ...	Tott., Bright., B. Stor. ...	Full	1643
Windmill, M. A. ...	Keeton's Road ...	Hom., Salis., Bright., Tru., Tott., H.&C., and 15 others	Too low, and no vacancy	1659
Keetley, L. ...	Blackheath Road ...	Tott.	Too low	1680
Little, C.	Silver Street ...	Tott., Oxf., Bris., Bright., Nor.	No vacancy ...	1685
Gibbons, S. ...	Haggerston Road ...	Hom., B. Stor.	Too low	1728
Moses, A. E. ...	Alexis Street ...	Stoc.	Too low	1783
Smith, E. ...	Holden Street ...	Stoc.	Too low	1800
Renton, S. ...	Belvedere Place ...	Stoc.	No room	1800
Macdonald, E. ...	James St., Westmr.	Hom.	Too low	1800
Harwood, E. ...	Addington Street ...	Stoc., Hom.	Too low	1819
Ross, L.	Berger Road ...	Stoc.	Too low	1819
Gowers, E. ...	Gainsboro' Road ...	Stoc.	Too low	1832
Miller, G. L. ...	Walnut Tree Walk ...	Stoc., Hom....	Too low. No vacancy	1833
Hope, J.	Shap Street... ...	Stoc., Darl., Swan., Glas., Edin., Tott.	Too low, and Colleges " full "	1853
Lilburn, E. ...	Albion Road ...	Hom., Swan., B. Stor., Bright.,Tru., Darl., Ripon	Too low, and no room	1856
Tyer, M. A. ...	New Park Road ...	Swan.	Too low	1863
Norwood, J. E. ...	Hatcham Park ...	Tott.	Too low	1876
Watson, Fanny ...	Wellington Street ...	Stoc.	Too low	1902
Wills, M. A. ...	Essex Street ...	Stoc.	Too low	1917
Howell, L. ...	Albion Street ...	Bright., Oxf., Nor.	Full	1919

NOTE *D*.
THE VICE-PRESIDENT OF THE COUNCIL ON TRAINING COLLEGES.

The changing attitude of the present Government relative to Training Colleges, may be gathered from various utterances, at different periods, of Mr. Mundella. On August 8th, 1881, Mr. Richard called attention to Training Colleges, in Committee of Supply (Hansard, vol. cclxiv., p. 1,306). The amendment of which he had given notice, but which he was prevented from moving by the rules of the House, was as follows :— " That the training colleges for elementary teachers, which are almost entirely maintained by public grants, and by the contributions of the students, should, so long as the present system of denominational training colleges exists, be open without sectarian restrictions to those candidates who, being otherwise qualified, pass the scholarship examination with the greatest success, and the same religious liberty should be accorded to them during their training which the law now secures to students at the Universities, grammar schools, and in public elementary schools throughout the country."

Mr. Mundella, in the debate, said (p. 1,325), " He confessed that the training college question had not occupied his attention. He was assured, however, that School Board teachers did go to the training colleges, 123 males and 224 females having passed through them according to the last return. He was told that legislation would be necessary on this subject, but that depended on the will of the House. He thought no teacher ought to be debarred from the training colleges on account of his or her religious opinions, and he was prepared to consider what was necessary to be done in the matter. If his honourable friend would give him a little time he would look into the question."

Mr. Illingworth said : " The Vice-President of the Council had not absolutely closed the door against his honourable friend (Mr. Richard), but he was bound to say his assurances were of a very vague character. . . . If it was found that some relaxation of the present tests was not conceded, he was certain that some radical change must be made in the direction of establishing training colleges against which the objection now urged would not lie."

On 21st March, 1882, Mr. L. Stanley, M.P. for Oldham, asked Mr. Mundella whether his attention had been called to a letter from the School Board for London, dated 27th January, 1882, addressed to the Education Department, complaining of the difficulties under which Board School pupil teachers labour in seeking admission to training colleges, and asking for relief, and whether he was prepared to propose any alteration which may secure full opportunities of training with protection for the rights of conscience to pupil teachers who have passed satisfactorily the scholarship examination, but who are excluded from college by the action of the college authorities and by their regulations. Mr. Mundella answered (Hansard, vol. cclxvii., p. 1,438) : " The letter is still under the consideration of the Department, together with the whole question of training colleges. The best way of securing the relief to which the honourable member refers is by increasing the accommodation in the undenominational colleges. The deficiency is mainly, if not exclusively, confined to the female colleges, and I am happy to be able to state that there are proposals now before the Department which will go far towards supplying it. I have had communications from the principals of the undenominational colleges for male teachers to the effect that they have already considerable difficulty in placing their students at the completion of their term, and that they are not desirous of increasing their number in training as the supply is already in excess of the demand."

On the 3rd of April, 1882, Mr. Lyulph Stanley had the following amendment on the paper : " That the existing system of training colleges being mainly under denominational management and the admission of students being entirely in the hands of the college authorities, is unsatisfactory and inadequate at the present day, as affording no protection to the rights of conscience of the students, and as tending to exclude those students who came from Board Schools who are desirous and well qualified to pursue the career of Elementary teachers ; and that the School Boards of this country which now educate a continually increasing proportion of all the children attending public elementary schools in England and Wales, are entitled for their teachers to an unsectarian system of training with the protection of a conscience clause." He called attention to the state of the training colleges and to the grievance of their irresponsible and denominational management.

Mr. Mundella (Hansard, vol. cclxviii., p. 624), replied. He said (p. 630) : " We cannot ask them (denominational training colleges), to admit persons of all faiths or of no faith into the family life of those colleges." . . . P. 631, he said : " Any person who is a fit subject to enter an undenominational training college and desires to enter it ought to have the right to receive that training." . . . . . (p. 632) " Further, I should be glad if I could see my way to establishing day training colleges in London. That, I think, would meet the whole case."

At Sheffield, Mr. Mundella said, in answer to a representation from the School Board, in January, 1883 (*School Board Chronicle*, Feb. 24th, 1883), " He was much obliged to them for bringing under his notice the letter from St. Peter's College, Peterborough, objecting to a candidate on account of his height. He thought a more unwise, he might say a more unworthy, regulation, he had never seen. He had no conception that any training college would object to receive an able and competent teacher simply because he did not reach a certain number of inches. They did not train their teachers for a military training, but for educational purposes. He should certainly bring this under the notice of the Department immediately on his return to town, and should address a remonstrance at once to the managers of the college on the subject. . . . He perfectly agreed with the deputation that it was deplorable that a teacher who stood high in the class list, and wished to go to a training college, should not have the same opportunity as a teacher of equal rank and standing who had not been trained in the Board school ; and he thought that where pupils were willing to conform to the requirements and observances of the training college it was taking a very extreme course to refuse admission. So far as these two cases were concerned, he went entirely with the deputation, and should be very happy to have instances given to him of any teacher, who, willing to go to a Church or Wesleyan training college, and willing to conform to the religious observances, was not allowed to enter such training colleges."

Mr. Mundella evidently recognises the evil complained of, but does not seem to be prepared to apply the only effectual remedy; for in the course of the same interview, he said, " That, whilst he was exceedingly anxious that the teachers, such as the Board spoke of, should have an opportunity of going in a training college, his first difficulty was with the training colleges. But when he came to the question of a conscience clause, and discussed it, everyone pointed out the utter impossibility of it. The Congregational college was just as much opposed to it as were the Roman Catholics or the Wesleyans. Those who went to colleges for instruction lived like members of one family, and they could not have a variety of people differing in their religious views brought together in that way. He understood that they did not object to that, but their objection was that the School Board teacher could not get in on the same terms. . . . At the same time I don't want to hold out to you the least idea that I can do anything at all to break up the distinctive or denominational character of the schools founded for that purpose."

Thus it will be seen that the Education Department so far, while to a certain extent recognising the grievance, endeavours to minimise it as much as possible, and while holding out vague hopes of remedial measures, has thus far done nothing, and yet, even without Parliamentary legislation, a modification of the Code would do much to remedy the more pressing injustice under which those who object to denominational training suffer.

P.S.—Since the above paper was written, and in type, the new report of the Education Department has appeared, which shows a further growth of the School Board system as compared with denominational schools.

Thus, in the year ending August 31st, 1882, the number of children in average attendance in Church of England schools was 1,552,973 out of 3,048,285, or less than 51 per cent. In Board schools, it was 951,896, or more than 31 per cent., and the greater efficiency of Board schools is shown by the fact that they earned 16s. 2d. a-head of grant compared with 15s. 8d. a-head grant in Church of England schools. In specific subjects, the superiority of Board schools is remarkable. The Board schools have an average attendance of about three-fifths of the Church schools, and yet they get more than 78,000 passes in specific subjects compared with less than 66,000 passes in specific subjects in the Church schools; had the Church schools got the same proportion of passes they should have got 130,000, or nearly twice as many as they gained.

www.ingramcontent.com/pod-product-compliance
Lightning Source LLC
Chambersburg PA
CBHW081309040426
42452CB00014B/2713